THE GOURMET BACHELOR

GLOBAL FLAVOR, LOCAL INGREDIENTS

Chad Carns

Photography by Sasha Gitin*
Design by Carns Concepts

Sasha Gitin, Photographer

Janine Kalesis, Food Stylist, Chef

Rob Fitzhenry, Chef

Justin Christoph, Wine Expert

*Lou Manna, Photographer
 Pages 70, 74, 93, 132

*Momo Attaoui, Chef, Food Stylist
 Pages 70, 74, 93, 132

Carns Concepts, Design Studio

ISBN-10: 0-615-22980-8
ISBN-13: 978-0-615-22980-5

Design by Carns Concepts

1 2 3 4 5 6 7 8 9 10

First Edition

THE GOURMET BACHELOR

GLOBAL FLAVOR, LOCAL INGREDIENTS

Chad Carns

Photography by Sasha Gitin*
Design by Carns Concepts

FLAVOR,

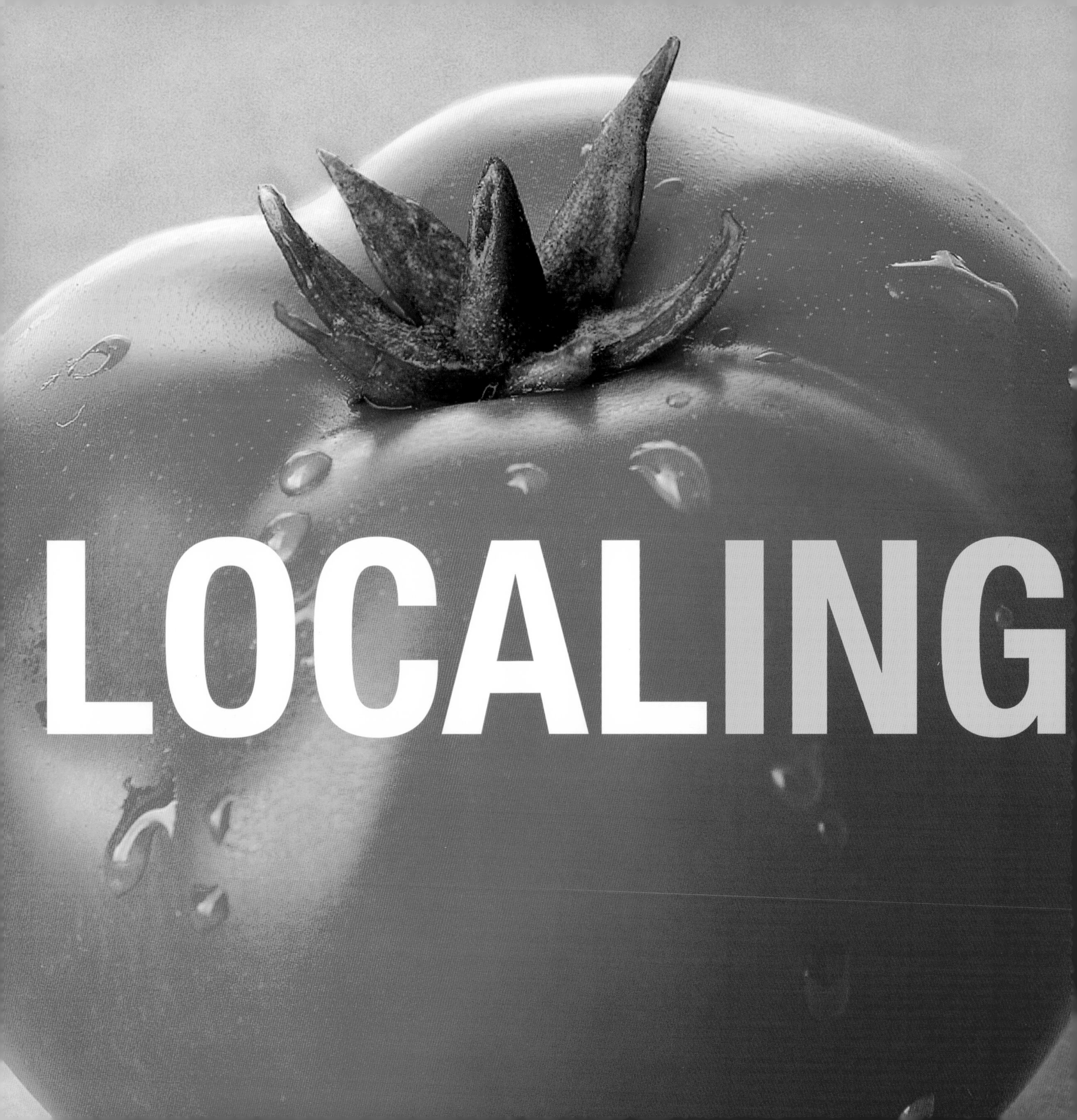
LOCALING

REDIENTS

BE INSPIRED by global flavor oozing
from the narrow streets of Greenwich Village.

WAKE UP to Ricotta Pancakes.
Ease into a Lobster Club, and slurp your way through Spicy Singapore Noodles. Then finish the night with warm Chocolate Soufflé.

breakfast lunch
tapas appetizer
salad noodle sushi
seafood chicken
duck pork lamb
steak dessert

WHAT'S GLOBAL FLAVOR?

It's the intoxicating aroma of garlic, lemon, wine and fresh basil oozing from the narrow streets of Greenwich Village. A spicy bowl of Singapore Noodles. It's an unexpected bottle of Moroccan wine paired with spicy Scallop Chorizo. And it's my commute every day from West 4th Street to Bleecker Street.

Prepare **1 MONTH** of quick, easy and intensely flavored global recipes with basic ingredients found in your local neighborhood market.

Learn **expert wine tips** and **essential cooking techniques.** Wine, beer, sake, small-batch bourbon — enjoy an expertly paired beverage for each dish.

1-51 INTRODUCTION

52-85 WEEK ONE

Ricotta Pancakes **Moroccan Chicken Wrap**
Wild Mushroom Cups Balsamic Reduction Scallop Ceviche
Argentine Steak Salad **Paella** Seared Spicy Tuna Roll **Mango Shrimp**
Honey-Glazed Salmon **Wild Striped Bass Zucchini and Fresh Herbs**
Balsamic Chicken Lamb Tagine **Parmesan-Crusted** Rack of Lamb
Chocolate Truffle Torte **Tres Leches**

86-119 WEEK TWO

Breakfast Quesadilla **Lobster Club** Tuna Ceviche Crisp Plantains Red Pepper Sauce
Lemon Sage Shrimp Greek Salad **Pad Thai** Italian Sushi Roll **Butter-Poached Lobster**
Spanish Tuna **Tomato Cod** Organic Chicken Tomato Wine Sauce
Coriander-Spiced Duck Breast Pineapple Relish Korean Steak Wrap
Tahitian Crème Brûlée **Chocolate Soufflé**

120-153 WEEK THREE

Frittata **Chicken Focaccia Sandwich Avocado Bacon Red Pepper Sauce**
Capri Bruschetta Scallop Chorizo **Polynesian Salad** Singapore Noodles
Tuna Mango Jalapeño Roll **Tequila Shrimp** Miso Black Cod **Almond-Crusted Tuna**
Chicken Masala Tuscan Stew **Venison Steak South African Wine Reduction**
Coconut Bread Pudding **Chocolate Tiramisu**

154-185 WEEK FOUR

Croque Madame **Pierogi Pizza** Crab Cakes Red Pepper Sauce Avocado Mash
Caribbean Crab Soup Tuna Mango Salad **Sausage Fennel Fusilli**
Spicy Tuna Alaska Roll **Tangerine Chili Shrimp** Potato-Crusted Sea Bass
Grilled Swordfish Saffron Cherry Tomatoes West African Chicken
Stuffed Veal Porcini Wine Sauce **Pork Tenderloin Pancetta Goat Cheese**
Chai-Spiced Cheesecake Green Tea Poached Pear

ODUCTION

I love restaurants. Great restaurants.
Not places with perfectly designed menus
to hide the dimly flavored food. I'm talking about
raw, pure, honest flavors. Places with menus
scribbled on a board. I want to see the chef
at my local market. I know his name.
And he knows my name.

COOKING TIPS

What do they do behind the doors of top kitchens?
Why are the dishes so flavorful? How do chefs achieve
that perfect sear?

I live in New York City. I can buy fresh ingredients. Sure,
it's nice to go out to trendy restaurants, but wouldn't it be nice
to enjoy your favorite dish at home?

Well, if you've ever asked yourself similar questions,
this book is for you. I welcome you to enjoy a few tips
that I picked up from top international chefs, wine experts,
and just personal experience.

HOW TO ACHIEVE THE PERFECT SEAR
JUST REMOVE THE SURFACE MOISTURE.

First, we must thoroughly **DRY THE MEAT.** If the meat is wet, we will never create a crust. The meat will steam until the moisture evaporates. Now we've got a soggy piece of overcooked meat. I use a paper towel even after a marinade.

HIGH HEAT is another way to create a golden crust. Turn your heat up to medium-high to create a crust. It will take an hour to get a crust on low heat.

Coat your meat with **FLOUR**. Again, we're removing the moisture by letting the flour absorb the outer moisture.

Another way is to buy a **QUALITY SAUTÉ PAN.** My dishes have drastically improved just by buying a single pan. A heavy, stainless steel or copper pan will conduct a consistent amount of heat without burning the dish.

Cook with **LESS OIL.** Too much oil and you're poaching the meat. Two tablespoons of olive oil will create the perfect sear for a fresh piece of sea bass

COOKING TIPS

know you might be saying, "What's up with this golden crust? My mother roasts a piece of meat for hours, and it's amazingly tender and moist." Yes, I know. But do you have 3 hours to roast a piece of pork? Go to a restaurant for slow-roasted meat. Or better yet, visit Mom.

INGREDIENTS

It's unnecessary to search for exotic ingredients in a specialty store to enjoy **global flavor.** You can find most of *The Gourmet Bachelor* cookbook ingredients in your local market. But it's important to **buy fresh ingredients.** Cooking can be easy if the ingredients already taste great.

SEASON (SALT & PEPPER)

This is probably the simplest and most effective way to make an average dish at home taste gourmet. Dishes at top restaurants taste great because the chef adds the perfect amount of seasoning.

My recommendation is to over-season your dishes at first. If you haven't over-seasoned a dish, you're probably not adding enough salt. I recommend generously seasoning your meat before searing. Most of the seasoning will fall off in the pan. If your health prohibits salt in your diet, I recommend trying salt-free alternatives to add flavor like citrus, fresh herbs and infused oil.

USE **FRESH, LOCAL** INGREDIENTS FOR EVERY RECIPE

WINE 101

JUSTIN CHRISTOPH HAS DEDICATED HIS LIFE TO WINE.

As a wine specialist for Christie's Wine Department, he helped procure a case of 1945 Mouton Rothschild Bordeaux that sold for roughly $345,000.* He traversed through a Spanish cave for a 1925 Rioja and threw the ultimate bachelor party in a Scottish castle packed with rare scotch.

But you'll also see Justin sipping on a perfectly poured pint of Guinness at his neighborhood pub.

Take advantage of Justin's passion for life and wine. Learn basic wine pairing tips and how to describe, order, store, and serve your favorite wine.

WITH JUSTIN

*Source: Peter D. Meltzer, "Christie's Shatters Auction Record Twice," www.winespectator.com, October 2, 2006.

TERROIR

The terror the word strikes in the hearts of the unsuspecting! Terroir is a term everyone likes to throw around these days to seem as though they know what they are doing. It's simply a French concept for where soil and climate come together at a specific location, making a wine a little bit different from that of their next-door neighbor and completely different from anywhere else in the world.

Grapes can be fickle and the slightest difference in environment can drastically change what's in your glass. The specific factors can be elusive, but at the end of the day, it's all about location, location, location.

VARIETAL

Think variety. This is just a fancy term for the type of grape. Just like apples and oranges, each one tastes different off the vine and has characteristics suited to making a specific type of wine.

WINE 101

BY JUSTIN CHRISTOPH

The skin of the grape gives wine its color and much of its flavor. When a grape tastes unfamiliar, we can describe it in terms of flavors we already know. Dark-skinned grapes can be described as: cassis-flavored and olivey Cabernet Sauvignon; soft, plummy Merlot; herb and blueberry-flavored Cabernet Franc; racy cherry-like Pinot Noir; smoky raspberry Syrah and earthy blackberry Grenache. Light-skinned grapes can be described as: oaky buttery ubiquitous Chardonnay, relatively neutral Pinot Gris (Grigio), zippy and grassy Sauvignon Blanc, minerally and versatile Riesling, perfumed Viognier, nutty Marsanne and spicy Gewürztraminer.

Many wines are a blend of different varietals even if only one type is listed on the label. Blending different grapes together can often make a finished wine that is greater than its parts as the grapes complement one another and balance potential shortcomings.

Beware of wine-soaked or dry, crumbling corks, which can be signs of an improperly stored wine that may have gone bad.

VINTAGE

This is the year the grapes were picked, not the year the wine was released, which can be the same year or up to several years later, depending on the winemaking process.

Choosing a vintage is not as complicated as one would think as ninety percent of all wines are meant be to be drunk young, so look for the youngest or most recent vintage. Some years are better than others, of course, depending largely on the weather. In general, vintages in Europe tend to be more variable than those in California and Australia. Wines that traditionally age well are the more structured reds and dessert wines.

It is best to consult your wine merchant, sommelier or trusted vintage chart for specifics, as each year is different. The weather can be different on each side of the road, meaning success or ruin for a given wine in its own little microclimate or terroir.

PRODUCER

Who made the wine? The person behind a wine is very important, but remember that you can make a bad wine from good grapes but not a good wine from bad grapes. Nonetheless, the producer, winery or domain (whatever you want to call it) leaves its finger-prints all over the wine, giving the wine its final form and style.

While nearly anyone can make at least a decent wine in a great vintage, only the best producers make some worthy to drink in difficult years.

Once you find one producer or winery you like in a given region, don't be afraid to try others with a similar style. It can be fun to try two similar wines side by side and see what the differences are or identify a unique characteristic of a particular producer in a blind tasting.

TANNIN

These prickly babies are the bitter quality in some red wines—a quality that is similar to the tight feeling you get on the side of your mouth when sucking on tea bags.

Classic wines with lots of tannin are Bordeaux and Cabernet Sauvignon, though most serious red wines have some amount of tannin to keep them in balance. Tannins are basically the structure, the flying buttresses and supports to the wine that help them age and stand up to fatty or rich foods. These and other wines may need to be opened early, prior to serving, often decanted, perhaps left in the cellar while a more forward, fruity wine is sacrificed.

BOUQUET (NOSE)

Aroma is the initial fresh grapy smell you get from a young wine. Bouquet is described by the secondary smells that wines develop, taking on similarities to other fruits and minerals. Generally, younger wines will have more primary aromas, developing bouquet in the glass the longer that they are open.

BALANCE

Balance is the sum of a wine's components and how they unfurl in your mouth. It's not any one thing in particular, but it is important and overlooked as a taster may be wooed by a wine that is over the top. A wine that is not balanced may smell good at first but will become progressively undrinkable and be difficult to match with many foods. If the wine is not balanced, you can compensate by matching it with certain foods whereas balanced wines will match a variety of cuisines.

The balance is constituted by the acidity, alcohol, sugar and tannins. Sugars play a larger role in white wines while tannins are largely the domain of reds.

Many wines are a **blend of different grapes** even if only one type is listed on the label.

DECANTING

Everyone likes to make a big deal about decanting. Basically, this is pouring the wine out of the bottle into another container: a carafe in a local bistro or a decanter in a fancy place.

The goal for reds and whites is to aerate the wine after it has been locked in the bottle devoid of oxygen for years or decades in suspended animation and to coax it into the atmosphere.

At the other extreme, very young, big wines may need decanting or double decanting (pouring back into the bottle after decanting) to shock them and round off their tannic edges to make them more drinkable. Red wines also contain a sediment (particles at the bottom of the bottle), that can be separated by simply stopping the pour into the decanter at the crucial moment. Nothing wrong taste-wise with the sediment. It's good for you. You can spread it on your toast in the morning.

TEMPERATURE

Temperature is often forgotten, though crucial to serving all types of wines. The temperature of the wine affects how the chemicals and molecules in the wine interact with the atmosphere as you drink it. Too cold, you can't taste anything, too warm and you taste things you would rather not, including the alcohol.

Popular wisdom is that lighter white wines are served the coolest and heavier red wines are generally served at the warmest temperature, but a word of warning: we tend to drink our white wines too cold and our red wines too warm. Room temperature means 65 F, "old world" room temperature, not the cozy 72 F we have been accustomed to. There's nothing wrong with putting a lighter red in a bucket of ice water for five minutes or even a more serious red that has been brought to you too warm at a restaurant.

CAN I ORDER THE SECOND CHEAPEST BOTTLE ON THE MENU?

Yes, but if you would like other inexpensive options, you can often get around naming a specific dollar amount by pointing to a bottle on the wine list and saying you want something similar, and it will be understood by a good waiter that you want a wine in that price range.

If there are several courses and you are on a date or with a small party, it can be less expensive and easier to match a glass of wine with each course. Have some fun with the sommelier by letting him or her have some fun and you may get a glass of dessert wine on the house.

WHAT TO ORDER AT A COMPANY DINNER

Ask what people are ordering and try to find a wine or several wines that will match. Don't try to order something too eclectic, obscure or over the top to impress. Stick to the classics and wines that you know

WINE ETIQUETTE

Ask the waiter or sommelier. They should know their list well, and if things don't work out exactly as planned, you can always blame them. When in doubt, order what your boss likes and come back another time to properly attack the wine list, glass in hand.

CORKAGE/RETURNING WINE

Return the wine because it has flaws, not because you don't like it, unless you feel that the sommelier or waiter has led you terribly astray with the taste of the wine or how it will match your food, a rare occurrence in our enlightened age. Be polite, of course, but firm in returning the wine as well as specific in the reason.

WHAT TO DO WITH THE CORK.

It's given to you to show that the wine in the bottle is the same as the one indicated on the label as demonstrated by the branding on the cork. Don't smell it. It smells like...cork. Do look for wine-soaked or dry, crumbling corks that can be a sign of an improperly stored wine that may have gone bad.

Actually, you should not be afraid to pair red wines with fish, particularly red meat fishes such as tuna and salmon. The problem that fish has with red wines is the tannins that clash and leave an off-putting metallic taste. Pinot Noir or a light Austrian red would be ideal with many fish dishes. A lot depends on the sauce regardless of the fish. The sauce acts almost as the intermediary and enzyme between the dish and the wine.

ITALIAN WINES PAIR WELL WITH ITALIAN FOOD...WHY?

Because that's what the locals drink. In general, Italian wines go well with Italian food because they are fairly acidic to contrast with rich hearty foods. The more traditional and noninterventionist a wine is, the more it can vividly convey a sense of place. Think more locally: Piedmontese wine with truffles from Alba and sturdy southern Italian wines with classic Sicilian dishes. In fact, most regions produce a tasty beverage that pairs perfectly with their local cuisine. Think sake with sushi or scotch with haggis. There is a conjoined evolution of food and wine as well as something indescribable in the air.

WINE PAIRING

OK, THEN WHAT TO PAIR WITH COMPLEX ASIAN FOOD?

Here we can break some of our own rules and go cross-cultural in the fusion of elements. Gewürztraminer is the standby, but sometimes can be too complex or powerful and fight with the food. Grüner Veltliner from Austria is often a more balanced complement to most Asian food with an off-dry Kabinet or Spätlese German Riesling faring better with spicier dishes as they have less alcohol and a hint of sweetness to soothe the burn.

WHAT'S UP WITH SWIRLING THE GLASS?

Swirling simply aerates the wine by stirring up molecules and allowing you to smell more of the good (and bad) things in a wine.

WINEGLASSES, HOW MANY DO I NEED?

Rather than traditional red or white division of labor, I recommend buying a set of six or eight relatively large, similarly sized Bordeaux and Burgundy shaped glasses. You can serve white or red in either glass depending on the grape.

A different shape for each is not necessary. You could serve Cabernet, Merlot and Riesling in the Bordeaux shaped glass and Syrah, Pinot Noir and Chardonnay in the Burgundy glasses. When in doubt, test your palate and the glasses. Try the same wine in both glasses before serving to see which is best.

When selecting a wineglass, avoid colored glass (or no glass at all) and décor that will distract your eye from the wine. Instead, look for long stems to keep your hand from warming the wine, large bowls to aerate the wine, and not too thick, preferably unleaded crystal. Ravenscroft is ideal—good value, difficult to break.

Glasses should only be filled about a third full so the wine can breathe properly and you can swirl without disaster looming. For a standard five ounce pour, you need glasses at least in the fourteen to sixteen ounce range. Never use soap to wash. The faintest hint can ruin wine. Rinse with the hottest water possible and dry with premium paper towels.

Besides that, all you need are pint glasses, martini glasses and a decanter for your basic glassware set.

I KNOW NOTHING ABOUT WINE. WHAT ARE THREE THINGS THAT I SHOULD REMEMBER?

Everyone says, "Drink what you like." What else? Find a good local restaurant with a list you can explore and a down-to-earth wine merchant who will give you sound advice, not just something with a brand name or a ninety point score. And if the recipes in the book pay off, you'll have a partner in crime to share tasting notes with.

ESSENTIAL CO

baking sheets
cast iron grill
cutting board
food processor
measuring cups
meat thermometer
pots

OKING TOOLS

sauté pans
sharp knife
spatula
sushi rolling mat
whisk
wooden spoon

ACKNOWLEDGMENTS

It's difficult not to be inspired by a city like New York. The energy, accessibility and life have made this book a reality. But it's the kind, talented, ambitious people who live here—with an uncompromising work ethic—that helped shape *The Gourmet Bachelor* cookbook into what it is today.

AJ, Murray's Cheese, you recommended the perfect artisan cheese pairing for my "Friday Nights In with Wine, Cheese, Dinner and Friends." **Ottomanelli Brothers,** your passion for quality meat has provided the foundation for every recipe. **Lobster Place,** your fresh quality seafood has made it easy to prepare simple gourmet dishes. **Asian grocery store on Bleecker and Morton,** you provided quality fresh ingredients from a space the size of a NYC apartment. **Aphrodisia,** thank you for providing thoughtfully selected spices in a welcoming way. **Jeff, Winesby,** you provided inspiration for every dish with your hand-selected boutique wine and from the inseparable story attached to every bottle.

Sasha, your passion for photography and dedication brought *The Gourmet Bachelor* cookbook to life. **Janine, Rob, Momo,** your food knowledge and work ethic influenced the culinary direction of *The Gourmet Bachelor* cookbook and your food styling made it visually amazing. **Lou**, your photography and guidance helped me realize that I could actually produce a quality cookbook. **Ed,** you've been a mentor and a friend. **Barry,** I met you at a focus group and you gave your photography equipment to me for two years. Thank You.

Justin, your wine knowledge took *The Gourmet Bachelor* cookbook to another level. **Aaron,** I don't know how you found time to develop and maintain thegourmetbachelor.com.

Every restaurant below 14th street, you provide a culinary explosion of taste, culture and excitement —I can travel to Thailand, Ethiopia, Peru, Italy and Spain within five blocks.

My family, from my earliest memory, I remember watching my grandmother mold one cup of flour, one egg and a splash of water into Sunday dinner. **My mother and father's** love for the celebration of food, family, friends and life will always be my inspiration. **Larry,** you pass three supermarkets on the way to your favorite butcher because the meat just tastes better—thank you! **Tracy,** you could have pulled the plug on any one of three 400-watt lighting heads in our living room that had doubled as a photo studio but you didn't. I couldn't have completed the book without your patience and encouragement.

Friends, somebody had to try the dishes. This book would have been a stack of recipes on my desk without you. You inspired me to take the book one step further everyday.

Special thanks to everybody who has helped to make this book a reality.

WEEK ONE

Ricotta Pancakes
Moroccan Chicken Wrap
Wild Mushroom Cups Balsamic Reduction
Scallop Ceviche Hot Chili Oil
Argentine Steak Salad
Paella
Seared Spicy Tuna Roll
Mango Shrimp
Honey-Glazed Salmon
Wild Striped Bass Zucchini and Fresh Herbs
Balsamic Chicken
Lamb Tagine
Parmesan-Crusted Rack of Lamb
Chocolate Truffle Torte
Tres Leches

52-85

RICOTTA PANCAKES

INGREDIENTS

2 c	instant pancake mix
3/4 c	water
8 oz	ricotta cheese
1/2 t	nutmeg
1/2 t	cinnamon
1 T	honey
1/2 t	orange zest

DIRECTIONS: Lightly mix together all ingredients. Pour 1/3 cup of batter onto a warm, buttered cast iron skillet. Cook until golden brown on each side.

Pairing: Bellini, Italy

Bellini: Add 6 oz peach puree to champagne flute. Fill with champagne.

MOROCCAN CHICKEN WRAP

INGREDIENTS

1 c	onion, chopped
1/2 c	butter
1 t	cumin
1 t	coriander
1/2 t	cinnamon
1/4 c	dried apricots, chopped
2 c	chicken broth
1 lb	boneless chicken
2 T	cilantro, chopped
1	phyllo dough package
2 T	honey
2 T	almonds, chopped

DIRECTIONS: Sauté onion in 1 tablespoon of butter for 3 minutes. Add cumin, coriander, cinnamon, apricots, chicken broth and chicken. Reduce heat. Poach until liquid evaporates. Shred chicken with a fork. Mix in cilantro.

Preheat oven to 350 degrees. Melt remaining butter. Brush 1 phyllo sheet with butter. Place 1 phyllo sheet on top of first sheet. Repeat. Place half of chicken mixture in the center of phyllo dough and roll like a burrito. Repeat. Bake both chicken wraps for 12 minutes. Garnish with honey and almonds.

Pairing: Cabernet Franc, Washington

WILD MUSHROOM CUPS BALSAMIC REDUCTION

INGREDIENTS

1 c	balsamic vinegar
4	garlic cloves, chopped
1/4 c	shallot, chopped
1 lb	wild mushrooms, chopped
2 T	olive oil
8 oz	mozzarella, shredded
1/4 c	Parmesan, grated
1 T	thyme, chopped
1 T	parsley, chopped
1/2 t	nutmeg
2 T	honey
30	phyllo dough cups
4 oz	goat cheese

DIRECTIONS: Preheat oven to 350 degrees. Reduce balsamic vinegar on low heat by half. Cool. In separate large skillet, sauté garlic, shallot and mushrooms for 8 minutes. Cool. Mix in mozzarella, Parmesan, thyme, parsley, nutmeg and honey. Spread phyllo dough cups out on a baking sheet. Spoon mushroom mixture into cups. Bake until golden brown. Top with goat cheese and balsamic reduction.

Pairing: Viognier, France

SCALLOP CEVICHE
HOT CHILI OIL

NGREDIENTS

	chili, thinly sliced
2 T	peanut oil
5	large scallops, cut into 1/4-inch slices
1 t	sugar
2 T	lime juice
t	sea salt
t	black pepper
t	lime zest
	radish, thinly sliced
T	scallions, thinly sliced

DIRECTIONS: Gently cook chili in peanut oil on medium-low heat
for 5 minutes. Spread scallops out on a serving platter. Mix sugar
and lime juice in a bowl. Pour over scallops. Flip scallops. Top with sea salt,
black pepper and lime zest. Spoon chili oil over scallops. Garnish with
radish and scallions.

Pairing: Fumé Blanc, Franco

STEAK SALAD

INGREDIENTS

Marinade
2 T	lime juice
3	garlic cloves, minced
1 T	honey
1 t	cayenne
1 T	oregano
1/4 t	cinnamon

Steak
1 lb	skirt steak

Salad
1 lb	romaine lettuce, chopped
1	ripe avocado, sliced
2	ripe tomatoes, quartered
1 T	balsamic vinaigrette

DIRECTIONS: **Marinade** – Mix ingredients. **Steak** – Marinate steak for 20 minutes. Grill steak until desired temperature. Remove and let rest. Slice against the grain in 1/4-inch strips. **Salad** – Mix ingredients. Top with steak

A smoking hot grill helps char the steak. A heavy stove top grill does the trick for my city apartment.

PAELLA

INGREDIENTS

1	chicken breast, 1-inch cubes
6 oz	chorizo, 1/4-inch slices
2 T	olive oil
1	onion, chopped
3	garlic cloves, chopped
1 c	rice
1/2 t	saffron
12 oz	can tomatoes, chopped
1 c	water
1 c	white wine
10	mussels, cleaned
10	shrimp, cleaned
2 T	lemon juice
6	lemon wedges
2 T	parsley, chopped

DIRECTIONS: Sauté chicken and chorizo in olive oil for 3 minutes per side. Remove. Sauté onion and garlic for 3 minutes. Add rice, saffron, tomatoes and water. Simmer for 15 minutes. Stir regularly.

Add wine, mussels and shrimp. Cover and cook for 6-8 minutes. Mix in lemon juice. Add chicken and chorizo. Serve with lemon wedges and top with parsley.

Pairing: Rioja, Spain

SEARED SPICY TUNA ROLL

INGREDIENTS

1/4 c	sesame seeds
1	egg
6 oz	sushi-grade tuna steak
2 T	peanut oil
6 oz	sushi-grade tuna, chopped
1 T	chili sauce
1 T	mint, chopped
1 c	sushi rice, cooked
2	nori sheets
1	bowl of warm water

DIRECTIONS: Spread sesame seeds out on a plate. Beat an egg in a bowl. Dip tuna steak in the bowl. Coat tuna with sesame seeds. Sear in peanut oil for 30 seconds per side. Remove.

Combine chopped tuna, chili sauce and mint. Cover sushi mat with plastic wrap. Dip your fingers into warm water. Spread half of the rice on top of sushi mat in an 8 X 8-inch square. Place nori on top of rice. Spread a layer of chopped tuna mixture in center of nori. Roll sushi and close. Repeat.

Slice tuna steak into thin slices. Wrap slices around top of sushi roll. Cut into 6 pieces. Repeat.

Pairing: Verdelho, Portugal

Sushi rice can be sticky. Dip your hands in a bowl of warm water when handling sushi.

Save time.
Buy sushi rice
from your favorite
take-out sushi
place.

MANGO SHRIMP

INGREDIENTS

1	mango, sliced
1	red pepper, sliced
1 T	ginger, minced
1/2	chili, minced
2 T	peanut oil
1 lb	shrimp, cleaned
1 T	honey
1/2 c	orange juice
8	basil leaves, thinly sliced

DIRECTIONS: Sauté mango, red pepper, ginger and chili in peanut oil for 4 minutes. Reduce heat. Add shrimp, honey and orange juice. Cook for 5 minutes. Add basil.

Pairing: Grüner Veltliner, Austria

HONEY-GLAZED SALMON

INGREDIENTS

2	salmon fillets

Marinade

2 T	peanut oil
2 T	soy sauce
2 T	honey
T	ginger, minced
c	pineapple juice
T	lime juice

Garnish

T	scallions, thinly sliced

DIRECTIONS: Marinade – Mix ingredients. Marinate salmon for 5-10 minutes. Sear salmon for 3 minutes per side. Add marinade to the pan and simmer for 2 minutes. Garnish with scallions.

Pairing: IPA Microbrew, Colorado

ZUCCHINI AND FRESH HERBS

INGREDIENTS

1	zucchini, round slices
3 T	olive oil
2	wild striped bass fillets
4	lemons, round slices
3 oz	thyme, parsley, tarragon
3 c	white wine
1/4 t	nutmeg

DIRECTIONS: Sauté zucchini in 1 tablespoon of olive until golden brown. In a separate skillet, sauté striped bass skin side up until golden brown. Flip fish. Place lemon and herbs on top. Pour in the wine and cover. Cook for 5 minutes. Place bass on a layer of zucchini. Dust with nutmeg.

Pairing: New Zealand Sauvignon

BALSAMIC CHICKEN

INGREDIENTS

c	balsamic vinegar
3 T	olive oil
T	parsley, chopped
lb	chicken breast, 1-inch pieces
/2 c	flour
3	garlic cloves, crushed
3 oz	mixed mushrooms
	lemon, halved

DIRECTIONS: Simmer balsamic vinegar for 20 minutes or until reduced by half. Cool. Blend 6 tablespoons of olive oil and parsley in a food processor. Dust chicken with flour. Sauté chicken in 2 tablespoons of olive oil for 3 minutes per side. Remove. Sauté garlic for 2 minutes. Add mushrooms and sauté for an additional 5 minutes. Spoon parsley oil onto white plate. Drip balsamic reduction onto plate. Add mushrooms and chicken to plate. Serve with lemon.

Pairing: Barbera, Italy

Tagine

1 lb	lamb, cubed
2 T	olive oil
1 c	onion, chopped
2	garlic cloves, minced
1 T	ginger, minced
2 c	skinless tomatoes, chopped
1/2 t	paprika
1/2 t	cinnamon
1/2 t	turmeric
1/8 t	saffron
1 c	water

Couscous

1/3 c	couscous
1/4 c	dried apricots, quartered
1 c	water
3 T	honey
2 oz	almond slices
1 T	cilantro, chopped

DIRECTIONS: **Lamb** – Brown lamb in olive oil. Remove. Sauté onion, garlic and ginger until translucent. Add remaining ingredients. Cover and then cook on medium-low heat for 20 minutes.

PARMESAN-CRUSTED RACK OF LAMB

NGREDIENTS

	rack of lamb
2 T	olive oil
2 T	Dijon mustard
/4 c	bread crumbs
/4 c	Parmesan cheese
T	thyme, chopped
T	parsley, chopped

DIRECTIONS: Preheat oven to 425 degrees. Sear lamb in olive oil until golden brown on both sides. Spread mustard over lamb. Mix bread crumbs, cheese and herbs. Spoon over lamb. Roast in oven until meat thermometer reaches 145 degrees.

Pairing: It's time to dust off that special bottle of Bordeaux.

CHOCOLATE TRUFFLE TORTE

INGREDIENTS

Torte

1 T	butter
2 1/2	sticks butter
10 oz	bittersweet chocolate (72 percent cocoa)
10	egg yolks
1 c	sugar, divided
1 t	vanilla extract
1/2 t	salt
9	large egg whites
1/4 t	cream of tartar
1	parchment paper sheet

Ganache

8 oz	bittersweet chocolate
1 c	heavy whipping cream
1 c	hazelnuts, chopped

DIRECTIONS: Torte – Preheat oven to 350 degrees. Coat 10-inch springform pan with 1 tablespoon of butter. Line bottom with parchment paper. Place chocolate and 2 1/2 cups of butter in metal bowl. Set bowl on top of saucepan with simmering water. Stir until smooth. Cool.

In a large bowl, beat yolks, 1/2 cup of sugar, vanilla and salt with an electric mixer until light in color. Fold in chocolate mixture. Whip egg whites with salt and cream of tartar. Slowly add remaining sugar once the egg whites become frothy. Whip until egg whites form soft peaks. Fold into the chocolate mixture. Pour batter into pan. Bake for 45 minutes. Cool torte for 20 minutes on a rack. Slide knife around torte's edge to loosen. Remove pan's sides.

Ganache – Place chocolate and cream in a metal bowl. Place bowl on top of saucepan with simmering water. Stir until smooth. Cool for 5 minutes. Spread 1 cup ganache over cake and freeze for 2 minutes. Pour remaining ganache over cake. Pack hazelnuts on side of torte. Chill cake for 1 hour.

Pairing: Banyuls, Catalonia

TRES LECHES

INGREDIENTS

1	prepared pound cake, 3-inch slices
1 c	sweetened condensed milk
1 c	evaporated milk
1 c	heavy cream
2 oz	light rum
16	strawberries, sliced
8 oz	whipped cream

DIRECTIONS: Arrange pound cake slices in an 8 X 8-inch pan. In a blender, combine wet ingredients, and then pour over cake. Spread strawberries over cake. Top with whipped cream and chill for 3 hours.

Pairing: Dark Rum, Puerto Rico

FRESH
LOCAL**ING**

REDIENTS

WEEK TWO

Breakfast Quesadilla
Lobster Club
Tuna Ceviche Crisp Plantains Red Pepper Sauce
Lemon Sage Shrimp
Greek Salad
Pad Thai
Italian Sushi Roll
Butter-Poached Lobster
Spanish Tuna
Tomato Cod
Organic Chicken Tomato Wine Sauce
Coriander-Spiced Duck Breast Pineapple Relish
Korean Steak Wrap
Tahitian Crème Brûlée
Chocolate Soufflé

86-119

BREAKFAST QUESADILLA

INGREDIENTS

2	tortillas
2 T	olive oil
1/2 c	red and green peppers, diced
1/4 c	corn kernels
4	eggs
2 oz	Cheddar cheese, shredded
1 T	cilantro, chopped

DIRECTIONS: Fry tortillas on each side. Remove. Sauté peppers and corn for 4 minutes. Whisk eggs. Stir eggs into skillet until fluffy. Add cheese and cilantro. Place egg mixture on top of one tortilla. Place second tortilla on top.

Pairing: Bloody Mary

Bloody Mary: Pour 2 oz vodka, 6 oz tomato juice, 2 dashes Worcestershire sauce and 1/2 fresh lemon over ice. Add hot sauce to taste.

LOBSTER CLUB

INGREDIENTS

1 lb	lobster chunks, cooked
2 oz	mayonnaise
4	white toast slices, buttered
4	bacon strips, cooked
6	avocado slices
4	tomato slices

DIRECTIONS: Mix lobster and mayonnaise in a bowl. Spread lobster mixture on top of 1 slice of toast. Top with 2 bacon strips, 3 avocado slices, 2 tomato slices and 1 slice of toast. Repeat.

Try Auslese Riesling, Germany. The sweetness of Auslese lifts the succulence of the lobster while the acidity cuts through the brininess.

TUNA CEVICHE
CRISP PLANTAINS
RED PEPPER SAUCE

INGREDIENTS

Ceviche

1/2 lb	sushi-grade tuna, cubed
1	avocado, cubed
1 T	chili sauce
1 t	cumin
1 T	lime juice
1 T	cilantro, chopped
1 bag	fried plantains

Red Pepper Sauce

1	roasted red pepper, peeled
4	garlic cloves
5 T	extra virgin olive oil
1 T	lemon juice
3 T	honey
1/2 t	cayenne pepper
1/2 t	cumin

DIRECTIONS: Ceviche – Mix ingredients. Cover and refrigerate for 15 minutes.
Spoon a dollop of ceviche onto a crisp plantain. **Red Pepper Sauce –**
Sauté peppers and garlic in 2 tablespoons of olive oil for 3 minutes.
Add remaining ingredients and blend in a food processor.
Top ceviche with red pepper sauce.

Pairing: Albarino, Spain

Can't find plantains?
Just use potato chips.

LEMON SAGE SHRIMP

INGREDIENTS

10	sage leaves
1 lb	shrimp, cleaned, dried
4 T	extra virgin olive oil
2 T	lemon juice
1 t	sea salt

DIRECTIONS: Spread sage leaves out on a serving dish. Sauté shrimp in 1 tablespoon of olive oil for 1 minute per side. Place shrimp on top of sage. Generously pour lemon juice and remaining extra virgin olive oil on shrimp. Sprinkle with sea salt.

Pairing: Trebbiano, Italy

GREEK SALAD

INGREDIENTS

Salad

2	cucumbers, 1/4-inch cubes
1/2	red onion, chopped
8 oz	cherry tomatoes, halved
6 oz	feta cheese, crumbled
2 oz	kalamata olives, pitted

Dressing

3 T	sugar
1 T	lemon juice
1/4 c	olive oil
2 T	dill, chopped

DIRECTIONS: **Salad** – Combine ingredients in bowl.
Dressing – Whisk ingredients. Pour over salad.

Pairing: Roditis, Greece

PAD THAI

INGREDIENTS

2 T	peanut oil
2	eggs, lightly beaten
4 oz	rice noodles, soaked in warm water then drained
2 T	lime juice
2 t	chili sauce
1/4 c	soy sauce
1/2 c	carrot, julienned
1 c	bean sprouts
1 c	cabbage, shredded
8	basil leaves
1 t	sugar

Garnish

1/3 c	peanuts, chopped
1 T	scallions, thinly sliced

DIRECTIONS: Heat peanut oil in a large skillet. Stir in eggs and noodles. Fry and stir for 2 minutes. Add remaining ingredients. Fry and stir for 4 minutes. Top with peanuts and scallions.

Pairing: Lager, Budvar

Spaghetti can be substituted for rice noodles in a pinch.

ITALIAN SUSHI ROLL

INGREDIENTS

1/4 c	balsamic vinegar
4 oz	prosciutto
2 c	sushi rice, cooked
6 oz	shrimp, cooked and cleaned
1 c	honeydew melon, sliced
1	bowl of warm water

DIRECTIONS: Simmer balsamic vinegar for 20 minutes or until reduced by half. Cover sushi mat with plastic wrap. Dip your fingers into warm water. Spread half of the rice on top of sushi mat in an 8 x 8-inch square. Place half of the prosciutto slices on top of rice. Layer half of the shrimp and honeydew melon across the square. Roll. Cut into 6 pieces. Repeat. Serve with balsamic reduction.

Arneise, a crisp, slightly sweet white wine from northern Italy, offers a perfect balance for the salty prosciutto.

BUTTER-POACHED LOBSTER

INGREDIENTS

Lobster

2 c	unsalted butter
2 (2 lb)	lobsters

Polenta

4 c	water
2 c	pre-cooked cornmeal
1/2 c	Parmesan
1/2 c	mascarpone
1/2 t	nutmeg

Shiitake Relish

4	garlic cloves, chopped
1/4 c	shallot, chopped
2 T	olive oil
8 oz	shiitake mushrooms, sliced
1 c	sweet corn
1 T	butter
3	thyme sprigs

DIRECTIONS: Lobster – Melt butter in a skillet on low heat. Place lobster in a 6-quart pot. In a separate pot, bring 4 quarts of water to a boil. Pour the boiling water over the lobster and cover. Steep for 5 minutes. Remove lobster from shell. Cook lobster in butter for 5 minutes. **Polenta –** Bring water to a boil, then slowly stir in cornmeal. Cook cornmeal for 3 minutes. Stir in remaining ingredients. Season and then cover. **Shiitake Relish –** Sauté garlic and shallot in olive oil for 3 minutes. Add mushrooms and corn. Sauté for 3 minutes. Stir in butter and thyme. Spoon polenta onto a serving dish. Add mushrooms, then lobster.

Pairing: Chardonnay, Meursault

SPANISH TUNA

105 THE GOURMET BACHELOR Global Flavor. Local Ingredients.

INGREDIENTS

2	yellow peppers, 2-inch slices
2 T	olive oil
1/4 c	honey
2 T	sherry
2	tuna steaks
2 T	fennel seeds, crushed

DIRECTIONS: Sauté yellow peppers in 1 tablespoon of olive oil until tender. Add honey and sherry. Carefully ignite sherry. Cook for 3 minutes. Coat tuna in crushed fennel seeds. In a separate pan, sear tuna in 1 tablespoon of olive oil for 2 minutes per side. Slice tuna into 1/4-inch pieces. Serve tuna with peppers.

Pairing: Zweigelt, Austria

TOMATO COD

INGREDIENTS

5	garlic cloves, crushed
1 c	yellow peppers, 1/4-inch slices
3 T	olive oil
28 oz	whole tomatoes, canned
1 t	red pepper flakes
1 c	water
8	basil leaves
2	cod fillets

DIRECTIONS: Sauté garlic and peppers in 2 tablespoons of olive oil for 5 minutes. Add tomatoes, red pepper flakes and water. Cook on medium heat for 15 minutes. Stir in basil. Sauté cod in 1 tablespoon of olive oil for 3 minutes per side. Serve cod on top of tomato sauce.

Pairing: Primitivo, Italy

ORGANIC CHICKEN TOMATO WINE SAUCE

INGREDIENTS

2	organic chicken breasts
1/4 c	flour
1/4 c	olive oil
1/2 c	onion, chopped
3	garlic cloves, chopped
	chopped tomato (very ripe)
2 c	white wine
1 T	tarragon, chopped

DIRECTIONS: Lightly coat chicken with flour. Sauté chicken in olive oil for 4 minutes per side. Remove. Sauté onion and garlic in olive oil for 3 minutes. Add tomatoes and wine. Reduce by half. Add chicken and continue to cook for 3 minutes. Top with tarragon.

Pairing: Vinho do Dão, Portugal

PINEAPPLE RELISH

INGREDIENTS

Pineapple Relish

1 c	pineapple, chopped
1 T	lime juice
1/4 c	red bell pepper. chopped
1 T	sugar
1 t	ginger
1 T	mint, chopped

Duck

2	duck breasts
1 T	coriander, crushed
2 T	kosher salt
2 T	peppercorns, crushed

DIRECTIONS: Relish – Combine ingredients. **Duck –** Score skin of duck in a diamond pattern. Rub coriander, salt and pepper over duck. Cook duck on low heat for 15 minutes skin side down. Flip and cook until desired temperature, roughly 15 minutes for medium. Let duck rest for five minutes

KOREAN STEAK WRAP

INGREDIENTS

Marinade

1/4 c	soy sauce
2 T	sugar
5	garlic cloves, minced
1 T	ginger, minced
2 T	sesame seed oil
1/4 c	water

1 lb	chuck blade roast

Garnish

2 T	sesame seeds
1/4 c	thinly sliced scallions
1 c	white rice, cooked
1/4 c	kimchi (optional)
6	lettuce leaves

DIRECTIONS: Whisk marinade ingredients together. With a sharp knife, slice roast in half horizontally. Cut straight down against the grain every 1/4 inch. Marinate the beef strips for 20-40 minutes. Cook on a smoking-hot grill for 2 minutes per side. Garnish with sesame seeds and scallions. Stack a scoop of rice, steak and kimchi onto each lettuce leaf.

Pairing: Cabernet Franc, Chinon

Inspired by a traditional Korean recipe provided by Yong Cha Stephens

TAHITIAN CRÈME BRÛLÉE

INGREDIENTS

1 c	heavy cream
1 t	Tahitian Vanilla extract
3	egg yolks
1/3 c	sugar
2 T	sugar

DIRECTIONS: Preheat oven to 325 degrees. Heat cream and vanilla over medium heat until steam rises, 5-6 minutes. Blend egg yolks and 1/3 cup of sugar in a bowl. Gradually blend hot cream into bowl. Divide among two 7-oz ramekins. Place ramekins into a 3-inch deep baking pan. Add hot water to fill pan halfway up the side of the ramekins. Cover with foil. Bake just until the crème brûlée is set, approximately 40–45 minutes. Remove the pan from the oven. Cool. Then chill for 3 hours. Just before serving, sprinkle each custard with 1 tablespoon sugar, then caramelize with a kitchen torch.

Pairing: Ice Wine, Finger Lakes

Try to find Tahitian vanilla. It will take you to the soft waters of Bora Bora.

CHOCOLATE SOUFFLE

INGREDIENTS

1 1/4 c	sugar
3 T	cornstarch
1 1/2	sticks of butter
1/4 c	brown sugar
3 oz	chocolate, 72 percent cocoa
4	eggs
3	egg yolks

DIRECTIONS: Mix sugar and cornstarch in a bowl. In a saucepan, bring butter and brown sugar to a boil, and then add chocolate. Stir until smooth. Add to dry ingredients. Whisk for 1 minute. Whisk in eggs and yolks. Chill overnight. Preheat oven to 375 degrees. Pour mixture into eight (6 oz) buttered ramekins and bake for 20 minutes.

Pairing: Cognac, France

ADD SALT & PEPPER
TO EVERYTHING

WEEK THREE

Frittata

Chicken Focaccia Sandwich Avocado Bacon Red Pepper Sauce

Capri Bruschetta

Scallop Chorizo

Polynesian Salad

Singapore Noodles

Tuna Mango Jalapeño Roll

Tequila Shrimp

Miso Black Cod

Almond-Crusted Tuna

Chicken Masala

Tuscan Stew

Venison Steak South African Wine Reduction

Coconut Bread Pudding

Chocolate Tiramisu

120-153

FRITTATA

INGREDIENTS

2 T	cream
6	eggs
4 oz	Monterey Jack cheese, shredded
1 T	butter
2 oz	chorizo, chopped
1 c	tomatoes, chopped
1/4	avocado, sliced

DIRECTIONS: Preheat oven to 400 degrees. Whisk cream and eggs. Add cheese. Melt butter over medium heat in an oven-safe skillet. Pour egg mixture into skillet. Stir and cook for 2 minutes. Add chorizo and tomatoes. Bake for 10 minutes. Top with avocado.

Pairing: Tempranillo, Spain

CHICKEN FOCACCIA
SANDWICH
AVOCADO BACON
RED PEPPER SAUCE

INGREDIENTS

Red Pepper Sauce

	roasted red pepper, peeled
4	garlic cloves
5 T	extra virgin olive oil
T	lemon juice
3 T	honey
/2 t	cayenne pepper
/2 t	cumin

Sandwich

2	boneless chicken breasts
2	6-inch focaccia squares
4	tomato slices
4	bacon strips, cooked
6	ripe avocado slices

DIRECTIONS: Red Pepper Sauce – Sauté peppers and garlic in 2 tablespoons of olive oil for 3 minutes. Add remaining ingredients and blend in a food processor. **Sandwich –** Grill chicken for 4 minutes per side. Slice focaccia in half. Grill. Assemble sandwiches.

Pairing: Ale, Scotland

Recipe provided by Tracy Carns

CAPRI BRUSCHETTA

INGREDIENTS

1	loaf Italian bread, 1/4-inch slices
1/2 c	extra virgin olive oil
3	ripe tomatoes, 1/4-inch slices, halved
10	basil leaves
16 oz	fresh mozzarella, 1/4-inch slices, halved
5	prosciutto di Parma slices, halved
1 T	salt
1 T	black pepper

DIRECTIONS: Grill bread for 1 minute per side. Remove. Drizzle half of the olive oil on toast. Stack ingredients on the toast. Season with salt and pepper. Drizzle with remaining olive oil. Finito!

Pairing: Rosso, Italy

SCALLOP CHORIZO

INGREDIENTS

1 c	potato, chopped
1/2 c	chorizo, chopped
1/2 c	onion, chopped
1 c	red and yellow peppers, chopped
1 T	parsley, chopped
2 T	olive oil
8	large scallops

DIRECTIONS: Sauté potato, chorizo, onion and peppers in olive oil for 8 minutes. Add parsley. In a separate pan, sear scallops on medium-high heat, 2 minutes per side. Serve scallops over chorizo and peppers.

Pairing: Ribera Del Duero, Spain

Serve with a sunny-side up egg for that Spanish flavor.

POLYNESIAN SALAD

INGREDIENTS

4 c	cabbage, shredded
1 c	red pepper, julienned
1 c	yellow pepper, julienned
8 oz	coconut milk
2 T	lime juice
1 T	chili
1/4 c	sugar
2 T	sesame seeds

DIRECTIONS: Combine ingredients. Toss. Place in refrigerator for 30 minutes.

Pairing: Lager, Thailand

Add chunks of fresh, sushi-grade tuna and you'll have poisson cru.

SINGAPORE NOODLES

INGREDIENTS

6 oz	glass noodles, cooked
/4	cabbage, sliced
/2	onion, sliced
T	butter
/2 lb	scallops
/2 lb	mussels
/2 lb	shrimp, cleaned
oz	coconut milk
6 oz	fish stock (or water)
T	curry powder
T	scallions, chopped

DIRECTIONS: Prepare noodles in boiling water according to package instructions. Drain. Sauté cabbage and onion in butter for 5 minutes. Add remaining ingredients (except noodles). Cover and cook on medium heat for 5 minutes. Ladle soup on a bed of noodles. Garnish with scallions.

Pairing: Semillon, Australia

For a spicy vegetarian alternative, remove seafood and add tofu

TUNA MANGO JALAPEÑO ROLL

INGREDIENTS

2 c	sushi rice, cooked
2	nori sheets
6 oz	sushi-grade tuna, cut into 1/4-inch slices
1/2	mango, julienned
1/2	jalapeño, julienned
1	bowl of warm water

DIRECTIONS: Cover sushi mat with plastic wrap. Dip your fingers into warm water. Spread half of the rice on top of sushi mat in an 8 x 8-inch square. Place nori sheet on top of rice. Layer tuna, mango and jalapeño on 1/3 of nori. Roll sushi and close. Repeat. Slice each roll into 6 pieces.

Sake pairs
nicely with sushi.
Not into sake? Try
Japanese beer.

TEQUILA SHRIMP

INGREDIENTS

Shrimp

1 lb	large shrimp, peeled
2 T	Old Bay seasoning
1 t	cayenne
1 t	cumin
2 T	olive oil

Sauce

4	garlic cloves, chopped
1/2 c	red, yellow and green peppers, chopped
1/2	chili, chopped
1/2	onion, chopped
2 c	tomato, diced
1/2 c	Anejo tequila
2 T	lime juice
1 T	cilantro, chopped

DIRECTIONS: Shrimp – Coat shrimp with spices. Sear for 2 minutes per side in olive oil. Remove. **Sauce –** Sauté garlic, peppers, chili and onion for 3 minutes. Add tomato. Pour tequila in a cup. Taste tequila. Remove pan from stove. Add tequila and then ignite. Wait for flame to dissipate. Add lime juice and shrimp. Top with cilantro.

Pairing: Anejo tequila, Mexico

To create a crusty outside and moist inside, dry the shrimp with a paper towel.

MISO BLACK COD

INGREDIENTS

1/2 c   mirin
1/4 c   sake
1 c   miso paste
1/2 c   sugar
2   black cod fillets

DIRECTIONS: **Miso:** Boil mirin and sake for 20 seconds. Stir in miso paste. Add sugar. Stir until dissolved. Cool. Coat black cod fillets with miso. Marinate for 20 minutes or up to 3 days in the refrigerator. Bake in a 400 degree oven for 10-15 minutes.

Pairing: Lagrein, Italy

ALMOND-CRUSTED TUNA

INGREDIENTS

Mushrooms

8 oz	shiitake mushrooms, sliced
1/2	shallot, minced
1 T	peanut oil

Tuna

1/2 c	almonds, crushed
2	ahi tuna steaks, 1-inch x 1-inch x 4-inch pieces
1	egg, whisked
2 T	peanut oil

DIRECTIONS: Mushrooms – Sauté mushrooms and shallot in peanut oil for 3 minutes. **Tuna –** Spread almonds out on a plate. Dip tuna in egg. Roll tuna in almonds. Place in refrigerator for 10 minutes. Sear tuna in peanut oil for one minute per side. Slice tuna into four 1-inch pieces. Place mushrooms on top of tuna. Serve with your favorite Asian dipping sauce.

Pairing: Pinot Noir, Oregon

CHICKEN MASALA

INGREDIENTS

1 lb	chicken breast, cubed
4 T	vegetable oil
1/2 c	onion, chopped
3	garlic cloves, chopped
1 T	ginger, chopped
1	cinnamon stick
1 T	garam masala
1 t	chili powder
2 T	tomato paste
4 T	yogurt
5 c	water
1 T	cilantro, chopped (garnish)

DIRECTIONS: Brown chicken on each side in vegetable oil. Remove.
Sauté onion, garlic and ginger for 3 minutes. Add spices. Stir in tomato
paste. Add yogurt, one tablespoon at a time. Add water. Simmer for 20
minutes. Add chicken. Garnish with cilantro.

ry Riesling with
picy dishes as
 has less alcohol
nd a hint
f sweetness
 soothe
e burn.

TUSCAN STEW

INGREDIENTS

1	onion, chopped
7	garlic cloves
1	shallot, chopped
2 T	thyme, chopped
4 T	olive oil
16 oz	tomatoes, chopped
2 lb	chuck roast, cubed
1 c	flour
2 oz	butter
3 c	white wine
1	rosemary sprig
1	cinnamon stick
3	cloves
2 c	carrots, cubed
2 c	potatoes, cubed

DIRECTIONS: Sauté onion, garlic, shallot and thyme in 2 tablespoons of olive oil for 3 minutes. Add tomatoes. Cook for 10 minutes on medium-low heat. Blend to a smooth consistency in a blender.

Lightly coat beef with flour. In a large, heavy pot, brown beef in butter and remaining olive oil. Remove. Deglaze pot with wine and reduce by half. Add beef, tomato sauce, rosemary, cinnamon stick and cloves. Simmer for 2 1/2 hours. Add carrots and potatoes. Cook for an additional 1/2 hour.

Pairing: Brunello, Italy

VENISON STEAK SOUTH AFRICAN WINE REDUCTION

INGREDIENTS

Wine Reduction

1	bottle of South African Pinotage
3 T	sugar
1 T	peppercorns, cracked
1 c	apples, cherries, plums; cut into large pieces
1	shallot, cut into large pieces

Mushrooms

8 oz	porcini mushrooms, sliced
2 T	olive oil
1 T	butter
1 T	thyme, chopped
4	garlic cloves, chopped

Steak

4	(6 oz) venison medallions
3 T	olive oil
4 T	butter
3	thyme sprigs
4	garlic cloves, smashed

DIRECTIONS: **Wine Reduction** – Simmer wine reduction ingredients until reduced to 1 cup of liquid, roughly 20 minutes. **Mushrooms** – Sauté mushrooms in olive oil for three minutes. Add butter, thyme and garlic. Cook for three minutes. Remove. **Steak** – Sear venison for 2 minutes per side in olive oil. Reduce heat. Add butter, thyme and garlic. Spoon butter over venison and continue to cook for 3 minutes. Serve venison on a bed of the wine reduction. Spoon mushrooms on top of venison.

COCONUT BREAD PUDDING

INGREDIENTS

Bread Pudding
3 c   milk
3 c   unsweetened coconut milk
1/2 c   sweetened coconut flakes
1   loaf French bread, 1-inch cubes
3   eggs
3/4 c   sugar
2 T   vanilla extract
1 T   butter

Mango Sauce
1   mango, peeled and sliced
1/2 c   sugar
1/2 c   water
1   vanilla bean, cut open

DIRECTIONS: Bread Pudding – Preheat oven to 350 degrees. Mix milk, coconut milk, coconut flakes and bread in a large bowl. Whisk eggs, sugar and vanilla extract in a small mixing bowl and then add to bread mixture. Grease a 13 x 9-inch baking pan with butter. Spoon the bread mixture into the pan. Bake on the upper rack of oven until the bread pudding has set and is golden brown on top, about 45 minutes. **Mango sauce –** Simmer ingredients for 10 minutes. Remove vanilla bean. Blend in a food processor until smooth. Serve pudding on a bed of mango sauce.

Pairing: Sauternes, France

CHOCOLATE TIRAMISU

INGREDIENTS

6	egg yolks
4 T	sugar
1 t	vanilla extract
16 oz	mascarpone cheese
1/4 c	brandy
1/2 c	espresso, brewed
24	ladyfingers
2 oz	dark chocolate, grated
2 T	unsweetened cocoa powder

DIRECTIONS: Beat egg yolks, sugar and vanilla until thick. Mix mascarpone into egg mixture. In a separate bowl, combine brandy and espresso. Dip ladyfingers in espresso mixture. Fit one layer of ladyfingers into an 8 x 8-inch glass baking dish. Spread half the mascarpone mixture on top of ladyfingers. Top with 1 oz grated chocolate. Repeat. Sprinkle cocoa powder on top. Refrigerate for 2 hours.

Pairing: Prosecco, Italy

MOST RECIPES YIELD TWO PORTIONS

WEEK FOUR

Croque Madame
Pierogi Pizza
Crab Cakes Red Pepper Sauce Avocado Mash
Caribbean Crab Soup
Tuna Mango Salad
Sausage Fennel Fusilli
Spicy Tuna Alaska Roll
Tangerine Chili Shrimp
Potato-Crusted Sea Bass
Grilled Swordfish Saffron Cherry Tomatoes
West African Chicken
Stuffed Veal Porcini Wine Sauce
Pork Tenderloin Pancetta Goat Cheese
Chai-Spiced Cheesecake
Green Tea Poached Pear

154-185

CROQUE MADAME

INGREDIENTS

3 T	butter
2 T	flour
1 1/2 c	milk
1/4 t	nutmeg
4 oz	Gruyère cheese, grated
4	thick bread slices
1 T	Dijon mustard
1/4 lb	ham, thinly sliced
2	eggs

DIRECTIONS: Melt 2 tablespoons of butter in skillet. Whisk in flour. Cook for 3 minutes on low heat. Add milk and whisk for 5 minutes. Stir in nutmeg and cheese. Remove. Spread cheese mixture on two slices of bread. (Save 2 ounces of cheese mixture.) Cover other pieces of bread with mustard and ham. Combine slices of bread to make two sandwiches. Fry in butter until crisp. Spoon remaining cheese mixture on top of sandwich. Broil until golden brown. Fry an egg. Place egg on top of sandwich.

Pairing: Côtes du Rhône, France

PIEROGI PIZZA

INGREDIENTS

8 oz	mashed potato mix
8 oz	bacon, chopped
1/4 c	onions, chopped
6	garlic cloves, minced
2 T	butter
1/4 c	flour
1 lb	pizza dough
4 oz	Colby-Jack cheese

DIRECTIONS: Prepare mashed potatoes as indicated on package. Sauté bacon for 4 minutes. Remove bacon and drain grease from pan. In the same pan, sauté onion and garlic in butter for 3 minutes. Add to mashed potatoes.

Dust table with flour. Roll out pizza dough in 4-inch circles. Spread mashed potatoes, cheese and then bacon over the pizza. Place pizza on a greased baking sheet or pizza stone. Place in a 500 degree oven for 10 minutes.

Pairing: Pilsner, Czech Republic

Save Time—Buy fresh dough from your favorite pizza place.

CRAB CAKE
RED PEPPER SAUCE
AVOCADO MASH

INGREDIENTS

Crab Cakes

1/4 c	red peppers, diced
1/4 c	corn kernels
1 T	olive oil
8 oz	crabmeat
1/4 c	bread crumbs
1	egg
1 T	mayonnaise
2 t	Dijon mustard
2 t	Old Bay

Fry

1/2 c	cornmeal
1/4 c	vegetable oil

Red Pepper Sauce

1	red pepper, roasted, peeled and quartered
4	garlic cloves
4 T	extra virgin olive oil
1 T	lemon juice
3 T	honey
1/2 t	cayenne pepper
1/2 t	cumin

Avocado Mash

2	ripe avocado, cubed
1 T	lime juice
1 T	cilantro, chopped

DIRECTIONS: Crab cakes – Sauté pepper and corn in olive oil for 3 minutes. Remove and cool. Mix with remaining crab ingredients to form small crab cakes. Coat with cornmeal. Fry in vegetable oil until golden brown.
Sauce – Sauté pepper and garlic in 2 tablespoons olive oil for 3 minutes. Add remaining ingredients and blend in a food processor. **Avocado –** Mix ingredients to a chunky consistency. Serve crab cakes on a bed of avocado and red pepper sauce.

Pairing: Chenin Blanc, California

CARIBBEAN CRAB SOUP

INGREDIENTS

1 c	sweet corn kernels
1/4 c	shallot, chopped
1 c	onion, chopped
1 c	celery, chopped
1	stick butter
1 T	cumin
1/2 t	cayenne
2 T	thyme, chopped
28 oz	tomato puree
14 oz	coconut milk
1 c	seafood stock or water
8 oz	lump crab meat

DIRECTIONS: Sauté corn, shallot, onion and celery in butter for 3 minutes. Add cumin, cayenne, thyme, tomato puree, coconut milk and seafood stock or water. Simmer for 40 minutes. Add crab and serve.

Pairing: Sherry, Manzanilla

TUNA MANGO SALAD

INGREDIENTS

Mango relish

1	mango, peeled, chopped
1	avocado, peeled, chopped
1/2	chili, sliced
1/4 c	orange juice
1 T	lime juice
2 t	mint, chopped
8 oz	organic greens
2 T	ginger dressing
1	yellow fin tuna steak

DIRECTIONS: Combine mango relish ingredients. Toss organic greens with dressing. Grill tuna for 2 minutes per side. Slice tuna thinly and layer around greens. Top with mango relish.

Pairing: Mojito

Mojito: Muddle 4 mint leaves & 1 teaspoon of simple syrup in a high ball glass. Add 1/2 lime, squeezed. Add 2 oz rum & ice. Stir. Top with soda water & mint.

SAUSAGE FENNEL FUSILLI

INGREDIENTS

1/2 lb	fusilli
4 oz	Italian sausage, sliced
2 T	olive oil
2 c	chicken stock
1/4 c	tomato puree
1 T	fennel seeds, crushed
8	sage leaves
4 T	canola oil
1/2 c	Parmesan, shaved

DIRECTIONS: Boil fusilli until al dente. Sauté sausage in olive oil until brown.
Add chicken stock, tomato puree and fennel seeds. Simmer 5 minutes.
Add fusilli. In a separate skillet, fry sage in canola oil until crisp.
Top with Parmesan and crisp sage.

Pairing: Amarone, Italy

SPICY TUNA ALASKA ROLL

INGREDIENTS

6 oz	sushi-grade tuna, chopped
1 T	chili sauce
1 T	mint, chopped
1 c	sushi rice, cooked
2	nori sheets
1	avocado, thinly sliced
6 oz	sushi-grade salmon, thinly sliced
1	bowl of warm water

DIRECTIONS: Combine tuna, chili sauce and mint. Cover sushi mat with plastic wrap. Dip your fingers into warm water. Spread half the rice, 1/4-inch thick, in an 8 x 8-inch square on top of sushi mat. Place nori on top of rice. Spread a thin layer of tuna mixture on top of nori. Roll sushi and close. Place a thin layer of avocado and then salmon on top of roll. Cut into 8 pieces. Repeat.

Cava, a sparkling wine from Spain, has the backbone to stand up to spicy tuna and the carbonation that blends nicely with the buttery texture of salmon and avocado.

TANGERINE CHILI SHRIMP

INGREDIENTS

2	garlic cloves, crushed
3 T	ginger, sliced
2 T	chili-garlic sauce
2 T	peanut oil
3 c	tangerine-orange juice
1 lb	shrimp, peeled
1 T	scallions, sliced

DIRECTIONS: Sauté garlic, ginger, and chili-garlic sauce in peanut oil for 2 minutes. Add tangerine-orange juice and cook for 3 minutes. Reduce heat. Add shrimp and cook for 4 minutes. Garnish with scallions.

Pairing: Gewürztraminer, Alsace

POTATO-CRUSTED SEA BASS

INGREDIENTS

Bass

	egg
2	sea bass fillets
c	instant potato mix
T	butter
T	olive oil

Cabbage

4 oz	bacon, chopped
2 T	butter
c	cabbage, julienned
/2 c	onion, julienned
2 T	tarragon, chopped
	lemon wedges

DIRECTIONS: Bass – Whisk egg. Coat bass with egg. Coat bass with potato mix. Sauté in butter and oil until golden brown.

Cabbage – Fry bacon until crispy. Remove bacon. Discard grease. Add butter to bacon pan. Sauté cabbage and onion 3 minutes. Add bacon and tarragon. Serve bass with cabbage and lemon wedges.

Pairing: Chablis, Burgundy

GRILLED SWORDFISH SAFFRON CHERRY TOMATOES

INGREDIENTS

2	swordfish steaks
4	garlic cloves, chopped
3 T	olive oil
10 oz	cherry tomatoes, halved
1/2 t	saffron
1 T	lemon juice
2 T	thyme, chopped

DIRECTIONS: Cook swordfish on a smoking hot grill for 4 minutes per side. Sauté garlic for 1 minute in olive oil. Add cherry tomatoes and saffron. Cook fo 5 minutes on medium-low heat. Top with lemon juice and thyme. Spoon sauce on top of swordfish.

Pairing: Carmenère, Chile

WEST AFRICAN CHICKEN

INGREDIENTS

1/2	eggplant, cubed
3 T	olive oil
lb	chicken breast, cubed
2	garlic cloves, crushed
	onion, chopped
T	ground cumin
T	ground coriander
T	crushed red pepper flakes
c	water
2 T	brown sugar
1/4 c	peanut butter
2 oz	cilantro, chopped

DIRECTIONS: Coat eggplant with 2 tablespoons olive oil and bake at 450 degrees for 15 minutes. Sear chicken in 2 tablespoons of olive oil until golden brown. Remove. Sauté garlic and onion for 3 minutes. Add cumin, coriander, red pepper, water, brown sugar and peanut butter. Cover and simmer for 10 minutes. Stir in chicken, eggplant and cilantro.

Pairing: Stout, Ireland

Inspired by a traditional Ghanese recipe provided by Karen Asaro's Mom, Juliana

STUFFED VEAL
PORCINI WINE SAUCE

INGREDIENTS

Veal
2 oz	prosciutto
4 oz	provolone
12	sage leaves
2	veal pieces, 8 x 8-inches, flattened
1 c	flour
3 T	olive oil

Sauce
1/2	shallot, minced
4 oz	porcini mushrooms, quartered
3 c	white wine
2 T	butter

DIRECTIONS: Place half of the prosciutto, provolone, and sage in center of veal. Roll veal and seal with toothpicks. Dust veal lightly with flour. Repeat. Sear in olive oil until golden brown. Remove. In same skillet, sauté shallot and mushrooms for 5 minutes. Add wine. Reduce by half. Add butter. Spoon sauce on top of veal.

Pairing: Barbaresco, Italy

PORK TENDERLOIN
PANCETTA
GOAT CHEESE

INGREDIENTS

8 oz	pancetta, cubed
1 T	olive oil
6 oz	goat cheese
	whole pork tenderloin
T	cumin
t	cayenne
t	cinnamon

DIRECTIONS: Preheat oven to 350 degrees. Sauté pancetta in 1 tablespoon of olive oil until crisp. Remove and cool. Stir pancetta into cheese. With a long, thin knife, slice a hole through the center of pork tenderloin. Stuff pork with cheese and pancetta. Seal with toothpicks. Coat pork generously with spices. Sear pork in remaining olive oil for 2 minutes per side. Bake pork until meat thermometer reaches 145 degrees.

Pairing: Pinot Noir, Burgundy

CHAI-SPICED CHEESECAKE

INGREDIENTS

Filling

16 oz	cream cheese
4 oz	marscapone
3/4 c	sugar
3	eggs
1	egg yolk
1 t	vanilla
1/2 t	salt
1/2 t	ginger, ground
1 t	orange zest
1/2 t	cardamom, ground
1	graham cracker pie crust

Topping

1 1/2 c	sour cream
3 T	sugar

DIRECTIONS: **Filling** – Preheat oven to 350 degrees. Using electric mixer, beat cream cheese, mascarpone and sugar in a large bowl until smooth. Beat in whole eggs one at a time, then yolk. Add remaining filling ingredients. Pour into pie crust. Bake for 1 hour. Cool. **Topping** – Beat ingredients with an electric mixer for 3 minutes. Spread on top of cheesecake and refrigerate for 1 hour.

Pairing: Tokaji, Hungary

GREEN TEA POACHED PEAR

INGREDIENTS

Pear

4 c	green tea, freshly brewed
1 c	sugar
1 oz	ginger, peeled and sliced
1	orange, quartered
1	sprig of mint
4	Asian pears, peeled and cored

Pistachio Cream Sauce

1 c	yogurt, drained
1/4 c	buttermilk
1 T	pure maple syrup
1 c	pistachios, chopped
2 T	orange peel

DIRECTIONS: Poached Pear – Place green tea, sugar, ginger, orange, mint and pears in a medium-size saucepan. Simmer for 20 minutes. Cool. Cover and place in the refrigerator overnight.

Pistachio Cream Sauce – Whisk yogurt, buttermilk and maple syrup. Place in the refrigerator overnight. Remove pears from poaching liquid. Spoon yogurt into pear. Garnish with pistachios and orange peel.

Pairing: Bourbon, Kentucky

GREENWICH VILLAGE FOOD TOUR

If you had one day to visit Greenwich Village, and you love interesting food without the attitude, where would you go?

SPECIALTY STORES

Astor Place Wine
399 Lafayette Street
Huge, quality wine selection

Lobster Place
252 Bleecker Street
www.lobsterplace.com
Fresh, exotic seafood and live lobster.

Murray's Cheese
254 Bleecker Street
www.murrayscheese.com
Ridiculous selection of artisan cheeses, cured meat and antipasti.
TGB Pick: Tomme Crayeuse (France), Meadow Creek Grayson (USA), La Tur (France), Sottocenere (truffle cheese, Italy)

Ottomanelli's Meat Market
285 Bleecker Street
Exotic meat at a reasonable price.

RESTAURANTS/WINE BARS

Bar Carrera
146 W Houston Street
Cozy Spanish tapas bar.

Lupa
170 Thompson Street
High-energy, rustic Italian restaurant.
Make reservations.
TGB Pick: Pork Shoulder

Meskerem
124 MacDougal Street
Cozy Ethiopian restaurant
TBG Pick: Vegetarian Combo

Noodle Bar
26 Carmine Street
Small noodle bar.
TGB Pick: Singapore Noodles

Check out a complete list of my favorite Greenwich Village restaurants and specialty stores at **www.thegourmetbachelor.com**

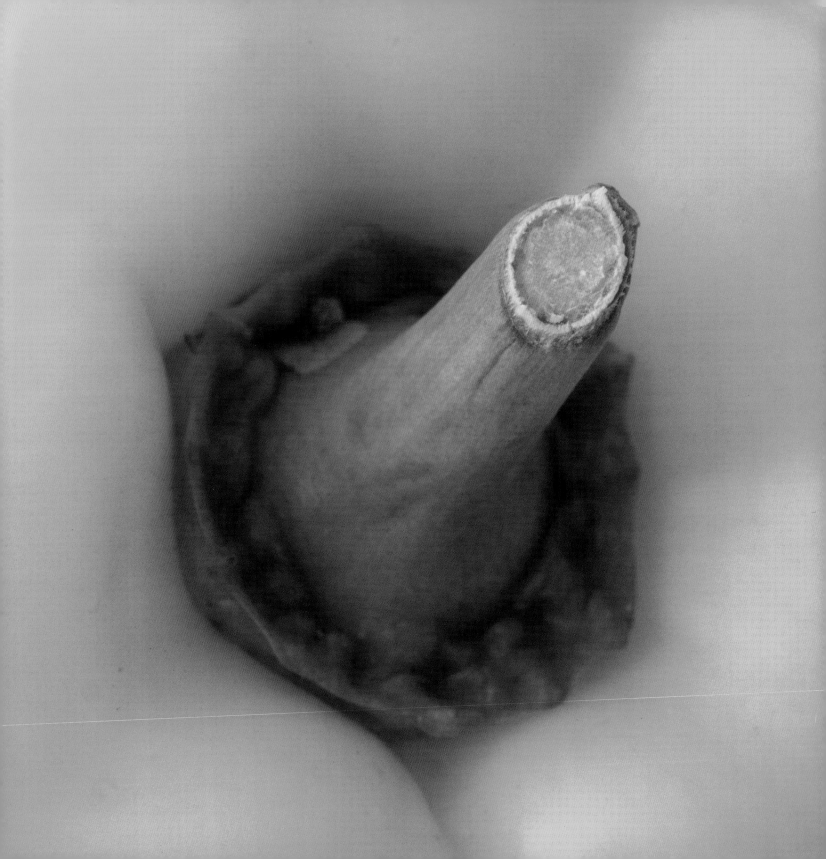

GOURMET RESOURCES

Momo Attaoui
Chef, Food Stylist
moattaoui@yahoo.com

Kendra Borowski
Food and Restaurant Publicist
kendrakicks@gmail.com

Carns Concepts
Restaurant Branding, Cookbook Design & Publishing
www.carnsconcepts.com

Justin Christoph
Bespoke Wine Services, The Barterhouse
www.winechristoph.com
www.thebarterhouse.com

Rob Fitzhenry
Chef, Food Stylist
rafnyc@gmail.com

SASHA GiTiN
Food Photographer
646.262.5686
www.sashagitin.com

Haus Interactive
Serving up fresh websites daily
www.hausinteractive.com

Janine Kalesis
Food Stylist / Recipe Developer
718.614.7505
www.janinestyles.com

Lou Manna
Food Photographer
www.loumanna.com

GOURMET COOKING TERMS

Bake
To cook food with dry heat.

Blend
To mix smoothly and inseparably together.

Brown
To fry, sauté or scorch slightly in cooking.

Chop
To cut into small bits.

Clean (Shrimp)
To peel and devein.

Crush
To break, pound or grind.

Dice
To cut into small cubes.

Fry
To cook in a pan or on a griddle over direct heat, usually in fat or oil.

Garnish
To decorate (prepared food or drink) with small colorful or savory items.

Grill
To broil on a gridiron or other apparatus over or before a fire.

Halve
To divide into two equal or equivalent parts.

Julienne
To cut into thin strips or small, matchlike pieces.

Marinate
To soak in a marinade.

Mince
To cut or chop into very small pieces.

Poach
To cook (eggs, fish, fruits, etc.) in a hot liquid that is kept just below the boiling point.

Preheat
To heat before using or before subjecting to some further process.

Quarter
To divide into four equal or equivalent parts.

Sauté
To fry briefly over high heat.

Sear
To char the surface of food to seal in the juices.

Season
To heighten or improve the flavor of food by adding salt.

Shred
To cut into small, narrow and long pieces.

Simmer
To cook in a liquid at or just below the boiling point.

Slice
To cut into thin, flat pieces.

Whisk
To whip (eggs, cream, etc.) to a froth with a whisk or beating instrument.

GOURMET INGREDIENTS

Cardamom
The aromatic seed capsules of a tropical Asian plant, of the ginger family, used as a spice.

Cayenne
Ground pods and seeds of pungent red peppers.

Cumin
A small plant, Cuminum cyminum, of the parsley family, bearing aromatic, seedlike fruit, used in cookery.

Fusilli
A type of pasta twisted into corkscrew or spiral shapes.

Garam Masala
An aromatic mixture of ground spices used in Indian cookery, usually containing black pepper, cardamom, cinnamon, cloves, coriander, nutmeg and turmeric.

Mirin
A sweet Japanese rice wine.

Miso Paste
A soy bean paste, which is an essential condiment in Japanese cooking.

Nori
A seaweed having a mildly sweet, salty taste, usually dried, used in Japanese cookery mainly as a wrap for sushi.

Saffron
The deep orange aromatic pungent dried stigmas of a purple-flowered crocus used to color and flavor foods.

Sake
A Japanese wine made from fermented rice.

Turmeric
A widely cultivated tropical plant of India, having yellow flowers, of the ginger family, used as a spice.

Temperature is measured in Fahrenheit

t = teaspoon
T = tablespoon
c = cup
oz = ounce
lb = pound
1 cup = 240 ml = 8 fl oz

1 stick of butter = 1/2 cup or 8 tablespoons

Uncooked food presents a higher risk of natural

SPANN VINEYARDS

GRAND VIN DE BORDEAUX

Château Cruzeau

SAINT-ÉMILION-GRAND CRU

APPELLATION SAINT-ÉMILION GRAND CRU CONTRÔLÉE

2005

SCEA Vignobles Luquot

EXPLOITANT A LIBOURNE, GIRONDE · FRANCE

MIS EN BOUTEILLE AU CHÂTEAU

750ml

RED BORDEAUX WINE   ALCOHOL 13 % BY VOLUME